The Music of Silence

ENTERING THE SACRED SPACE OF MONASTIC
EXPERIENCE

David Steindl-Rast, O.S.B.,
with Sharon Lebell

HarperSanFrancisco
A Division of HarperCollins*Publishers*

ACKNOWLEDGMENTS

Special thanks are due John Loudon, Executive Editor at HarperSanFrancisco, who conducted the conversations on which this book is based and then edited the resulting manuscript through its various stages; and to Nancy Graeff, who generously gave of her time and skills to meet a tight editorial schedule.

Angel musicians by Fra Angelico, from the Tabernacle of the Linaioli, Museo di San Marco, Florence, Italy. Courtesy of Scala/Art Resource, New York.
Epigraphs from Abraham Joshua Heschel, *I Asked for Wonder: A Spiritual Anthology*, edited by Samuel H. Dresner (New York: Crossroad, 1990), 4 and 10.
Grateful acknowledgment for permission to reprint poetry by Denise Levertov.
From *Candles in Babylon,* © 1982 by Denise Levertov. Reprinted by permission of New Directions Publishing Corporation.
Chant © 1994 Angel Records.

Book design by Jaime Robles

FIRST EDITION

ISBN 0-06-067589-6 (cloth)
ISBN 0-06-067451-2 (pbk with CD)

95 96 97 98 99 ❖ HAD 10 9 8 7 6 5 4 3 2 1

This edition is printed on acid-free paper that meets the American National Standards Institute Z39.48 Standard.

THE MUSIC OF SILENCE

CONTENTS

HE WHO HAS REALIZED that sun and stars and souls do not ramble in a vacuum will keep his heart in readiness for the hour when the world is entranced.

For things are not mute:

the stillness is full of demands, awaiting a soul to breathe in the mystery that all things exhale in their craving for communion.

Out of the world comes the behest to instill into the air a rapturous song for God . . .

ABRAHAM JOSHUA HESCHEL

[The] Syntax of Silence:

OUR AWARENESS OF GOD is a syntax of the silence in which our souls mingle with the divine, in which the ineffable in us communes with the ineffable beyond us.

It is the afterglow of years in which soul and sky are silent together, the outgrowth of accumulated certainty of the abundant, never-ebbing presence of the divine.

All we ought to do is to let the insight be and to listen to the soul's recessed certainty of its being a parenthesis in the immense script of God's eternal speech.

ABRAHAM JOSHUA HESCHEL

A NOTE ON GREGORIAN CHANT

GREGORIAN CHANT IS A VAST COLLECTION OF music, made up of about three thousand chants. Each chant, whether it be a psalm, hymn, or prayer, consists of a single melody, sung either by a soloist, by the choir, or responsively between a cantor and the choir. No instruments accompany the music and it is sung in free rhythm. The music follows the flow of the words.

Gregorian chant grew over many centuries and is widely believed to be derived from Jewish chant, since its earliest forms can be traced to Palestine and Syria. Pope Gregory I, who presided over the Roman Catholic Church from 590 until 604, commanded that a way be found to collect and preserve this sacred music.

The oldest manuscripts containing chant melodies date from the tenth century and are notated in special signs called neumes. The neumes indicated whether a melody was heading up or down in pitch, and the manner in which a given chant was to be performed.

It was in the early Middle Ages that Gregorian chant, which was flourishing within the Holy Roman Empire, assumed what is today considered its traditional form (though later musical innovations developed). In the nineteenth century, amid much controversy over what Gregorian chant should really be, the Benedictine monks at the Abbey of Solesmes, in France, embarked on a century-long effort to restore the chant to its medieval traditional form. Working with original manuscripts found all over Europe, they established the proper interpretation of hundreds of chants.

Every day, the world over, the chants are sung by monks during the canonical hours, the public service of praise and worship *(officicium* or *Opus Dei)* that takes place at appointed times each day. The canonical hours—Vigils (Matins), Lauds, Prime, Terce, Sext, None, Vespers, and Compline—are divided into the three major choral offices: Vigils, Lauds and Vespers, and the "Little Hours"—Terce, Sext, None, and Compline. Some monasteries combine certain of the hours, like Vespers and Compline, into a single office, and many now omit Prime altogether.

It is the chant from this centuries-old tradition that we now hear in the album *Chant*, sung by the Benedictine Monks of Santo Domingo de Silos.

THE
SEASONS
OF THE
DAY

THE QUIET ECSTASY OF GREGORIAN CHANT CALLS to people of all faiths. What is its timeless fascination? The chant speaks to our hearts today because it is a universal call to enter the *now:* to stop, to listen, and to heed the message of *this* moment. It speaks to the monk in each of us, to our soul, which longs for peace and connection to an ultimate source of meaning and value.

Saturated with information but often bereft of meaning, we feel caught in a never-ending swirl of duties and demands, things to finish, things to put right. Yet as we dart anxiously from one activity to the next, we sense that there is more to life than our worldly agendas.

Our uneasiness and our frantic scrambling are caused by our distorted sense of time, which seems to be continually running out. Western culture reinforces this misconception of time as a limited commodity: We are always meeting *dead*lines; we are always short on time, we are always running out of time.

Chant music, on the other hand, evokes a different relationship to time, one in which time, while precious, isn't scarce. It conjures the archetype of the monk's way of life, wherein time flows harmoniously; the time available is in proportion to the task at hand. The pure, serene, yet soaring sounds of the chant remind us that there *is* another way to live in this noisy, distracted world, and this way is not as out of reach as it might seem.

When listening to the *Chant* album, we become aware not only of the blended voices of the monks, but also of an almost inaudible echo, an additional dimension of depth to the music. It is this sacred, transcendental quality of the melodic lines, chanted in a high-ceilinged oratory, that many find so appealing about Gregorian chant. And it is this depth dimension that is so much like the *now* dimension of time. For now does not occur in chronological time, but transcends it. Here, time is not conceived as running out, but as rising like water in a well, rising to that fullness of time that is now. It is to that centered, present living in the now that chant calls us.

The chant proclaims a harmony, wholeness, and healthiness that calls us to wake up from uneasy workaday scheming and tension; to let go of our wooden, publicly constructed self and drop down into our true self. It is a straightforward invitation to our souls to wake up from defensive cynicism, to choose a different way, to stop chattering: to listen.

THE MONASTIC UNDERSTANDING of the word "hour" goes back to a Greek word, *hora,* which is older than our notion of a day broken up into twenty-four-hour segments. The original notion of hour is something quite different from a unit of time composed of sixty minutes. It is not a numerical measure; it is a soul measure.

We come closer to an appreciation of the original meaning of hour when we reflect on the seasons of the year. They betoken the original understanding, in which a season is a mood and an experience, not an exact period that starts, say, on the twenty-first of December and ends on the twenty-first of March. In fact, we're usually surprised when we find in the calendar that the first day of winter is the twenty-first of December, because either winter has long been here, or it's not yet winter at all. It's rare that any season really starts on its assigned date. Rather, seasons are qualitative experiences: We sense a subtle difference in the quality of light, the length of daylight, the feel of the air on our skin. We know intuitively that something is happening in nature.

The hours are the seasons of the day, and they were originally understood in a mythical way. Earlier generations of our human race, not ruled by alarm clocks, saw the hours personified, encountered them as messengers of eternity in the natural flow of time growing, blossoming, bearing fruit. In the unfolding rhythm of everything that grows and changes on earth each hour had a character and presence infinitely richer and more complex than our sterile clock time. As messenger from another dimension—an angel as it were—each hour was understood to have its own significance.

Today, even in our busy city schedules, we notice that predawn, early morning, mid-morning, and high noon each have qualities all their own. Mid-afternoon, the time the shadows lengthen, has a different character from the time when it gets dark and we turn on the lights.

A canonical hour thus is more a presence than a measurement. The hours that call the monks together for prayer and chant are angels we encounter at different points in the day. The hours are called canonical, since the word "canon" originally meant a measuring rod, and it is by its different moods that the day is measured. But canon can also mean a trellis, like a lattice that supports vines. So we can also think of the canonical hours as the frame by which the monastic day, indeed the monastic life, is supported.

The hours are the inner structure for living consciously and responsively through the stages of the day. The monastic relationship to time through the canonical hours sensitizes us to the nuances of time. And as this sensitivity deepens, we become more available to the present moment.

The responsive singing of chant in each hour helps monks to find the elusive now dimension of our lives. Chant primes us to respond to the call of each hour; for real living happens not in clock time, not in chronological time (from the Greek *chronos*), but in what the Greeks called the *kairos,* time as opportunity or encounter. From the monastic perspective, time is a series of opportunities, of encounters. We live in the now by attuning ourselves to the calls of each moment, listening and responding to what each hour, each situation, brings.

The canonical hours are the seasons of the monastic day in another sense as well. The word "season" comes from a Latin root meaning "to sow," and it also means a station or a stage. So the hours of the day are the stations or phases of the day when we sow certain seeds within ourselves and outside in the world. The seeds we sow are the virtues appropriate for each hour.

When we step out of mere clock time, in which we simply react, we enter instead into the seasonal time of the day's hours by responding consciously to the message of a particular hour's angel. Each of the monastic hours issues a distinctive challenge and calls for a unique response. And this message-response interplay is itself symbolically expressed by the antiphonal structure of chant.

Calling and responding belong to the very essence of this music. Chant is not a solo performance, it's a choir performance. And it's the whole community that chants, not just specialized singers. What matters is not the singer but the song, the self-transcending responsiveness that chant demands.

The rule of St. Benedict—the "trellis" (for rule is *canon* in Greek), the latticework that has supported Western monastic life for 1,500 years—reminds monks that they stand in the presence of angel choirs whenever they chant. And they sing like the angels, who are said to be calling one another, answering one another in never-ending praise. That is also an expression of spiritual life as a whole, which is, in its essence, a life of love, of listening and responding to God and to one another. Love is not a solo act.

In CHANT, WHICH IS not so much an acoustic phe-nomenon as it is an inner experience, we encounter a reality that is more real than what we experience in our daily, busy lives. Why is this so?

One of the reasons we feel so ill at ease in our daily lives is that we are either ruminating about the past, or worrying ahead into the future, and thus we are not present in the here and now, which is where our real selves reside. When we feel we are not real, we are like T. S. Eliot's "hollow men." Chant calls us out of chronological time, in which "now" can never be located, and into the eternal now, which is not really found *in* time.

If we envision time as a line that leads from the future into the past, then the past is continuously eating up the future without the least remnant. As long as we think of "now" as a very short stretch of time, nothing prevents us from cutting that stretch in half, and half again. Because chronological time can always be further subdivided, there is no "now" on our clocks, no "still center" to be found in clock time. To think of time in this way is not just to play with words; it's a mental experiment we can do to bring

11

home to ourselves that, in knowing what now means, we are experiencing something that transcends time: eternity.

Eternity is not a long, long time. Eternity is the opposite of time: It is no time. It is, as Augustine said, "The now that does not pass away." We cannot reach that now by proceeding in mere chronological sequence, yet it is accessible at any moment as the mysterious fullness of time.

We are welcomed into time's mystery once in a while in our most alive moments, in our peak experiences. We say of those moments, "Time seemed to stand still," or "So much was crammed into one little moment," or "Hours passed and it seemed like just a flash, a second." Our sense of time is altered in those moments of deep and intense experience, and so we know what now means. We feel at home in that now, in that eternity, because that is the only place where we really *are*. We cannot *be* in the future and we cannot *be* in the past; we can only *be* in the present. We are only real to the extent to which we are living in the present here and now.

THE MONASTIC VENTURE IS commonly misunderstood as an effort to be super-pious, to be more holy than other people. But the rationale for monasticism could be most succinctly described as an effort to live in the now. The monastery is a place in which everything is arranged so that it is made easy to be here now. And one way of achieving that is to follow the natural rhythm of the hours of the day.

As a monk, ideally speaking, you always know what you're supposed to do at a given time. The moment when the bell rings for an activity, you drop whatever you have in your hands and turn to this new activity in readiness and responsiveness: because that hour is like an angel who calls you and challenges you and wants your response at that moment. Even though this is made easier in the monastery, the attitude behind it is something that people in any walk of life can attempt to realize. And, to the extent to which they realize it, it will make them happy.

The poet Rainer Maria Rilke traveled in Russia at the turn of the century and was deeply impressed by the monastic life that he found there. Like so many people who personally have no inclination or vocation to become monks, this young man of twenty-five was nevertheless deeply impressed by the archetype of the monk. He wrote a series of poems that he called *The Book of Hours,* the title taken from the book from which monks chant the canonical hours.

The very first poem in this collection speaks of the hour announced by the monastic bell as bending down and touching the poet who exclaims, "My senses tremble." Our senses may tremble when we open ourselves and allow an hour, a time that is ripe for us, to really touch us.

The bell wakes us up to the now, and it challenges us to do what it is time for, because at every moment it is time to do something, even if it is just time to sleep. An ancient motto says, *"Age quad agis."* "Do what you're doing." There's liberty in truly doing what you are doing. Obedience is not constraint, it is loving listening, and readiness to respond. This loving response to the call of a given moment frees us from the treadmill of clock time and opens a door into the now.

Chant teaches us something else about living in the present. From a pragmatic point of view, chant is a useless activity, it doesn't accomplish anything. We are so geared to what is useful that we forget the meaningful, what gives our life joy and depth and value. To listen to music or to sing a chant is to do something that has no practical purpose; it is just celebration and praise; it is just tasting of the joy and beauty of life, the glory of God. Listening to it, even in the midst of a very purposeful day, reminds us to add the other dimension to our experience, the dimension of meaning, that makes it all worthwhile.

To engage with chant can produce a kind of sober ecstasy. Ecstasy literally means to stand outside of oneself. When we are chanting, or listening to chant, we are reaching into that dimension that is out of time, into the now. Paradoxically, we transcend clock time precisely by standing in the instant, literally, standing in the present moment. The instant and ecstasy belong together: When we are truly present here, now, in this instant, then quite spontaneously we also are ecstatic.

T. S. Eliot speaks of "music heard so deeply that it isn't heard at all, but you are the music while the music lasts." And he sees in this experience an aspect of "the moment in and out of time." When we learn to combine the two and live "in and out of time," we turn the polarity between time and now, between instant and ecstasy, into a creative tension. This inner gesture allows us to live full and creative lives.

INVOLVEMENT WITH CHANT instills in us that inner gesture of listening and response, which we can then apply to any activity in the course of the day. Yet while we long for the wholeness and harmony that come from being fully present to our moments, at the same time we are afraid of it. Wherever we experience the pure call of the moment, whenever we are confronted with stark reality, we tremble. We are used to living on the everyday air of compromise and muddling through, and suddenly we are challenged to breathe pure oxygen and we are afraid we are going to burn up. That is why Rilke says, "Every angel is frightening." And yet what could be more beautiful than an angel? Supreme beauty is not pretty. It's the beauty of an electric storm: It thrills us, and it frightens us. "Beauty," Rilke tells us, "is but the beginning of terror which we can just barely sustain, and we admire it so, because it serenely disdains to destroy us."

We long for an encounter with the angel; we long for a genuine encounter with reality and yet, at the same time, we are afraid of it, just as we are afraid of the overpowering experience of falling in love. We flee from it, and yet we are irresistibly attracted by it.

T. S. Eliot observes, "Humankind cannot stand very much reality." Why is it that we are afraid to live in the now?

We are afraid of becoming real, just like the toys in the children's book *The Velveteen Rabbit.* They all want to become real—that is the great dream of toys. But they are afraid, so they ask one of the more experienced toys, "Does it hurt to become real?" That is the same fear we have. Does it hurt to encounter reality? As the old toy wisely answers, "When you are real, you don't mind that it hurts."

Opus Dei, the monks call it, when they chant the hours of their monastic day; *opus Dei*: the work of God.

When we are in love, singing our lover's praises is not work. Neither is chant. Gregorian chant is heartfelt praise. While at times it can be a cry of anguish, an expression of our need, it always retains the overtones and the undertones of praise. Praise is our response to the glory of God—to the shining forth of God's presence in everything, every person, and every situation. The more loving we are, the more we see that glory shining forth. The more we see it shining forth, the more our spontaneous reply is praise. This is what humans are made for. We are by nature those who sing praise. That is our highest goal.

The monastic life is often called the contemplative life. Contemplation doesn't just have to do with concentrated periods of meditation. Contemplation literally means a continuous putting together according to some measure.

But what are we putting together in the contemplative life? We're connecting the two realms with which we have been dealing in these pages: chronos and kairos. When we live the contemplative life, we continuously measure what we are doing in time against the now that doesn't pass away. We strive continuously to tune in to God's creative Spirit, God's will, God's plan, and to let it give shape to reality "on earth as it is in heaven."

Contemplative life is the putting together of vision and action. Vision alone, meditation alone, is not true contemplation. We must put vision into action. Not just monks, but all of us are called to contemplation in this full sense. If we want to live healthy lives, we have to build into our daily life moments of vision, and then let our action be formed by that vision. Listening to chant can be a moment in which we open our inner eyes to the vision that needs to be enacted.

Traditional Christian spirituality speaks of looking at everything *sub specie aeternitatis,* which means looking at things from the point of view of eternity. In ordinary life, we are tempted to measure things subjectively: in terms of earthly success, achieving our goals, or fulfilling someone else's expectations. But our lives have depth and meaning only when we view them from a higher vantage point, when we measure our temporal concerns against the eternal now. That now reverberates in chant.

We know that achieving our goals only on the pragmatic, material, temporal (and thus temporary!) level is not what makes us really happy. What gives us deep, abiding joy is finding ourselves at home where we really are, fully alive and present in the now. But who can stay for long in that blessed realm? We like to think that the great masters of the spiritual life, the great ascetics, can do so. Maybe.

An ancient story from the very beginning of Christian monastic life makes this point well: A young monk travels to an old, highly respected monk way out in the Egyptian desert and tells him that he keeps losing his peace of mind. The young monk wants to find a recipe to preserve his inner peace. To his great surprise, the old man replies, "I have worn this habit for seventy years and not in a single day have I found peace."

If even that seasoned monk finds that the peace of the moment is constantly assailed, what are we to say? What counts is not that we have this peace as a firm possession, but rather that we never cease to strive for it. Perfection is not achievement; perfection lies in untiring striving.

CHANT SEEMS PERFECT, even though it's performed by nonprofessional singers. It's part of the genius of the music that anyone can learn to be part of the choir.

Chant is a folk art: Its imperfection is part of its perfection. It accommodates all kinds of voices and vocal skills; in the monastery, chant is sung by whoever happens to be there and enters into its shared spirit. Imperfections are therefore inevitable, as they are in life. And this is the point: A remarkably transcendent beauty is generated when ordinary people, with their shortcomings, give themselves to the chant.

Chanting is an integral part of all the religious traditions—Buddhist, Jewish, Hindu, Islamic, and others. This is because at a certain pitch of religious experience, the heart just wants to sing; it breaks into song. Paradoxically, you could say when the silence finds its fullness, it comes to word. As the Book of Wisdom says, "When night in its swift course had reached its half-way point and deep silence embraced everything"—when night was at its darkest and deepest—there "the eternal Word leaped from the Heavenly throne": silence burst into song.

THIS BOOK IS A JOURNEY through the hours of the monastic day. To hear the music of silence and to hearken to its message, we must step out of clock time into the monastic flow of time as expressed through the hours of the day. We must forsake our usual unconscious gesture of *reaction*, and make the aware inner gesture of *response* to what is before us in each moment. With this inner attitude, we will meet the angel of each hour and come to an understanding of the seeds the angel calls us to sow, the virtue the hour calls us to develop in our own lives.

VIGILS

—

THE NIGHT WATCH

VIGILS IS THE WOMB OF SILENCE, THE LONGEST hour.

Walking to the oratory under the predawn starry sky is an awe-inspiring experience and a fitting beginning for the monastic day as the monks gather for Vigils.

They enter the monastery's heart, the oratory, while it is still dark. The oratory is a place dedicated to only one purpose: prayer. At this hour, the only light will often be that of the cantor's lectern. The choir sits rapt in darkness. All details are hidden.

Out of this womb of darkness and silence emerges the chant.

Vigils—also known as Matins—is the night watch hour, the time for learning to trust the darkness. Looking up to the night sky, we are reminded of the immense mystery in which we are immersed.

The root meaning of the word "mystery" is to shut one's eyes and ears. Mystery is silence, darkness. Rilke speaks in his *Book of Hours* of turning inward, of looking deep into himself, and he reports what he finds: "My God is dark." He sees a thousand theologians plunging like divers into the night of God's name.

The poet prays, "You darkness from which I come, I love you more than the flame that sets boundaries." The shining flame lights up the things around it, but outside of this arbitrary circle of light lies deep darkness, which is limitless. That darkness is symbol and image for the divine mystery, the nothingness (the no⁄thing⁄ness) of the divine realm. Everyday reality, the world of things we learn to manage, is inherently finite, bounded, lit up, and delim⁄ited.

But darkness holds everything, embraces everything, in⁄cluding you and me. "And maybe in this darkness a great energy stirs right near me," the poet says, and then expresses his deepest conviction: "I trust in night."

Vigils is an invitation to learn to "trust in night," to trust the darkness despite the immense fear it triggers. We have to learn to meet mystery with the courage that opens itself to life. Then we discover, as the Gospel of John puts it right in the prologue, "The light shines in the darkness." This doesn't mean that light shines *into* the darkness, like a flashlight shining into a dark tent. No, the good news that the Gospel of John proclaims is that the light shines right in the midst of darkness. A great revelation: the very darkness shines.

This is why the Psalmist sings: "I will say to that dark-ness, 'be my light.'" To recognize the darkness itself as light can be a great consolation. When we find ourselves in inner darkness, we cry out with the prophet, "Watchman, what of the night?" When is it going to be over?

The challenge is to look deeply enough to discover that this darkness is all that we need, and to find in it what we are looking for. Listening deeply to chant, we will hear a darkness turned into sound, a darkness that shines.

The night wind is the natural voice of Vigils. Wind is a symbol for spirit, which comes from the same word as breath or breathe. The Holy Spirit is that life breath that blows in the darkness. Chant is the spirit made audible. It's a symbol for the wind that blows in the mind, and we can-not tell "whence it cometh and whither it goeth." It is a total surprise, total creativity.

To sing chant, monks learn to breathe correctly; by learn-ing to breathe, one learns to be centered and to be more pre-sent where one is. In one of his poems, Robert Frost whimsically speaks of the wind that didn't yet know how to blow until we humans took it in and gave it voice. Chant, like poetry, is the wind the wind was meant to be: "The aim was song."

WE ALL STRUGGLE with dark periods, like Jacob wrestling in the night with the Divine Presence in the form of a dark angel, beautiful and yet terrifying. At the end of the night, the angel says, "Let me go." But Jacob replies, "I will not let you go unless you bless me." As dawn breaks, the angel blesses him, but also injures him by touching his thigh. From that day on, Jacob limps. There is a mysterious woundedness that somehow goes with great blessing.

When we truly encounter the night in all its beauty and terror, we have no assurance whatsoever that we are going to come out unscathed. If you come out injured, it might just be a sign of the blessing that you have received there.

THE HOUR OF VIGILS is also a symbol of the waking up we have to do in the midst of our lives. The kind of world in which we live is really a benighted world. This watching in the night and waiting for the light, this wakefulness, is a forceful reminder to wake up throughout the day from the world of sleep to another reality. A daydream, a chance remark overheard, a fleeting thought that crosses our mind as we wait in the express lane at the supermarket, may be the message of an angel, passing as swiftly as a shooting star in the night sky. Time to wake up.

THE ANGEL FOR VIGILS wears a dark scarlet garment and holds his horn as if he were ready to blow, but he is not yet blowing. His left hand makes a strange gesture that signals, "Wait; not yet." His eyes are turned upward. He waits in that reverent silence out of which every genuine sound must come. This angel personifies the expectant listening attitude that must precede genuine word or song.

VIGILS CALLS US to a loving listening. Because we have so much restlessness and noise in us, we find it hard to nurture a listening attitude. So even the very listening to chant begins cultivating that listening. It is an attentiveness that begins with our sense of hearing but leads much further and much deeper. Monks are encouraged to listen with their hearts so that in the end they may perceive "what eye has not seen, nor ear heard."

Rising well before dawn for Vigils allows monks to add a whole extra dimension to their day. Not a few men and women outside the monastic life have discovered that they, too, can bring the spirit of Vigils into their lives by setting aside a certain time and space for nothing but spiritual pursuit: meditation, prayer, silence, listening to music—whatever suits them.

If we add a little time to the beginning of our day, even if it means getting up fifteen minutes earlier, this contemplative moment in the early morning can enrich our whole day. Don't worry, you're not wasting time. Don't think that you are taking time away from something that needs to be done. Without the contemplative dimension, the whole day can slip away into a mad chase, but those few minutes can give it meaning and joy. And if you can set aside a little corner in your home, however modest, as a sanctuary, that space can readily conduct you each day back into the contemplative mode.

We are such efficiency experts that we think there's no room for the superfluous; whatever is extra should be cut out. And yet it is superfluity, overflow in the word's literal sense, that gives spark and glory to our lives.

Affluence is exactly the opposite. The word affluence suggests that whatever flows in never comes out. Our affluent society stays affluent by making the containers bigger when they are just about to overflow, like a fountain with its lovely veils of water spilling over. The economics of affluence demand that things that were special for us last year must now be taken for granted; so the container gets bigger, and the joy of overflowing, gratefulness, is taken away from us. But if we make the vessel smaller and smaller by reducing our needs, then the overflowing comes sooner and with it the joy of gratefulness. It's the overflow that sparkles in the sun.

The less you have, the more you appreciate what you've got. With the extraneous stripped away, you begin to realize how you are being graced by life's gifts. That is at least one sense in which the poor are blessed.

Nothing is more needed in our lives than superfluity, because only with overflow is there joy. Therefore, nothing is needed more than frugality. When your needs are limited, your vessel is easily filled, and you can delight in the overflow.

Monks experience the overflow sooner; poor people experience it sooner than wealthy ones, because the vessel is smaller. With monks, who by custom have few and simple possessions, it is artificially made smaller, and so the joy of overflowing comes sooner. If you normally have just soup for your meal, and all of a sudden you get a second course of potatoes, that feels like a wonderful gift, a blessing, and you are thrilled.

If you get up fifteen minutes earlier, you have this extra bit of time that doesn't have to be put to some practical purpose. The useful fits into your normal routine. You can delight in this extra time, savoring it in any way you wish. Many play music in the morning. Not a few these days listen to chant, the music that monks chant at this hour, music in which the great silence of mystery becomes sound. If you make time for this, it may change the whole character of your day.

Vigils, then, is the hour that calls us to set aside time outside the practical demands of the day and to connect with that dark but grace-filled mystery in which we are immersed. Once the bright light of day dawns and the demands of the day begin, it is easy to forget the sacred, timeless dimension of our lives. The angel of Vigils challenges us to carry through the rest of the day the mystery of a darkness that gives light; to carry it with wonder and joy, like a melody we cannot forget.

LAUDS

—

THE
COMING OF
THE LIGHT

Harper San Francisco
ATTN: KATHLEEN MCNULTY
1160 Battery Street
San Francisco, CA 94111-1213

*H*arper San Francisco is a general publishing house whose books explore spiritual, philosophical, and psychological questions. If you would like to know more about our books, please complete this card and mail it to us. We will be pleased to send you a catalog.

_____
Name (please print or type)

_____
Street

_____
City

_____
State   *Zip*

_____
Title of the book in which you found this card

BFN

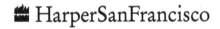 HarperSanFrancisco

THE MONASTIC HOUR OF LAUDS TAKES US OUT of the darkness, into the light. At Lauds we receive the new day as a gift at sunrise. Vigils saw us through the celebration of the darkness and the encounter with the dark infinity of night; now we celebrate light.

Rilke has a beautiful poem in *The Book of Hours* that could have been written especially for Lauds. It is almost a little creation myth. The poet hears God speaking to each of us before we are born, before we are fully made, in the womb of darkness. Then God is going forth with us out of the night. "Sent forth by your senses," God directs us, "go to the very edge of your longing and clothe me." The way we deal with the mysterious silence and darkness from which we come is the way God will find expression in the world. Each one of us is destined to express the divine mystery in a unique way.

Then God says, leading us into the light, "Let everything happen to you, beauty and terror. No feeling is the furthest out. Do not let yourself be cut off from me." And in parting, God tells us, "Near is the land that is called life. You will recognize it by its seriousness. Give me your hand." This new land into which we are sent is God's gift: the one great gift, the gift of life itself, the gift of being.

The angel of Lauds has a brighter robe than the angel who watched over Vigils. The outer garment is still dark, but out of it comes the rosy dawn color with the gold of the sun's first rays. This angel is looking up attentively, ready to clang the cymbals, but not yet making a sound. The angel is alertly looking for the cue to clash the cymbals: sunrise, the breaking forth of full light.

THE GIFT WITHIN every gift is always opportunity. Most of the time, it is the opportunity to rejoice and to delight in the moment. Not often enough do we pay attention to the many opportunities we have each day simply to enjoy: the sun shining through the trees, dew glistening on a just-opened flower, the smile of a baby, the embrace of a friend. We can sleepwalk through life until something comes that we cannot enjoy; only then are we startled awake. If we were to learn to avail ourselves of those countless opportunities to enjoy, to dwell in the gift of being alive, then, when the moment comes to do something difficult, we could see that, too, as an opportunity and gratefully take advantage of it.

Life is given to us; every moment is given. The only appropriate response therefore is gratefulness. When we wake up to the fact that everything is a gift, it is only natural to be thankful and to look on everything that happens as a chance to respond to the Given Life. That awareness seems particularly appropriate to evoke at the opening of the day, and that is precisely what the chant of that hour invites us to do.

Its music soars; it is a chant of joy and a chant of gratefulness. That celebratory sense of gratefulness and delight continues to run through the chant for the rest of the day, even when it is more measured and restrained. Whatever part of chant we listen to, we can hear this deep joy resonating in it, because joy is appropriate even in the midst of suffering, even in the midst of pain.

Joy is that kind of happiness that doesn't depend on what happens. Normally, we are happy when something good happens, and we are unhappy when something happens that we do not consider good. We pick and choose. But joy is our wholehearted response to whatever opportunity is given to us in any moment. It does not depend on what happens.

If we cultivate this grateful joy, which finds its voice in chant, we can be happy no matter what happens. We sometimes get this wrong. We think that people are grateful because they are happy. But is this true? Look closely, and you will find that people are happy because they are grateful. When we are thankful for whatever is given to us, no matter how difficult, no matter how uninvited it may be, the thankfulness itself makes us happy. Saints teach us this: They're full of humble thanks for whatever life brings them. Of course, that attitude is often difficult to adopt when suddenly we're faced with a trying, even tragic situation. But if we start with easy things, then the habit of gratefulness will gradually become second nature: Do we have eyes to open to the morning light? Do we have ears to listen to the sounds, and feet to walk and lungs to breathe? What gifts! Should we not be thankful and delight in them?

LAUDS, THEN, STARTS US OFF with the attitude that the day is a gift, that everything in our life is a gift—allowing us to see that the appropriate response to this given world is gratefulness.

I always associate Lauds with the high oratory windows. When the Lauds chanting begins on a winter morning, they are still completely dark. But as the light dawns, the panels begin to show their colors, their images and designs shining forth. Those monastery windows, as night becomes day, are for me a vibrant image of what happens when we open our eyes with gratitude to anything that comes our way: We see the divine light shining through everything that is.

Someone may say, "Well, yes, but how can I be grateful for the massacres in Rwanda? How can I be grateful for the terrorism in the Middle East?" And even closer to home, how can we be grateful for the misery in our streets? The devastation of our environment? The torture of animals in labs and in factory farms? We cannot be glad for those things in and of themselves, but we can be thankful for the opportunity to do something about them. This full response to the gift of the present moment is an enormously creative inner stance. It inspires us to see what we can do, however little it may be. At least we can ask what it is we can do. Let us take advantage of this opportunity. If enough people ask, "What can we do?" we will eventually find solutions to our most pressing problems.

The sunrise can be a reminder of the day's gift because it comes unbidden. We don't produce it. The light is given. The world is reborn each morning, and we are given a whole new time of opportunity. Even if the difficulties are the same as we had yesterday, we can tackle them in a new way. This fresh outlook is what the Buddhist monks call "beginner's mind."

The opportunity to adopt this attitude is not restricted to monks: It is open to everyone. As Rilke says, again in *The Book of Hours,* "Nothing was completed before I laid eyes on it." What I see no one else has ever seen before; not with my unique vision, not from my unique point of view. I am a creator of each new day. I am given the opportunity with this new light to see, to appreciate, to respond, as the person I uniquely am.

What a gift each morning to encounter some part of nature. We may have never paid full attention to it: the morning sky, the trees waving in the wind, birds singing, flowers blooming. Nature is just there; it has no immediate utilitarian value; it is a pure gift of beauty, of life. As Gerard Manley Hopkins says, "There lives the dearest freshness deep down in things." And primordial freshness is renewed each morning.

Denise Levertov captures the joyful surprise at this freshness in a poem that seems to be specially written for commuters. It starts with all the difficulty, tension, and negativity of a commuter's morning. Then, as if by chance, the eye catches a glimpse of beauty. If we allow ourselves to dwell on that sight, no longer than it takes to read the second stanza, our heart will be lifted up by this soaring poem as it can be lifted up on the musical wings of chant.

Each day's terror
almost a form of boredom——madmen
at the wheel and
stepping on the gas and
the brakes no good——
and each day one,
sometimes two, morning glories,
faultless, blue, blue sometimes
flecked with magenta, each
lit from within with
the first sunlight.

The opposite of gratefulness is just taking everything for granted. As long as we go around taking things for granted, we will never see the light; reality remains opaque, like the monastery windows before the sunshine transforms them into walls of light. But to the extent to which we allow surprise to flow into our lives, our whole life becomes translucent. Surprise is not yet gratitude, but with a little bit of goodwill it grows naturally into gratefulness.

A friend's young daughter said to him one morning, "Dad, isn't it amazing that I exist?" Children know intuitively how surprising and delightful it is that there is anything at all. And the child in us never dies. We can lock it up, we can forget it, and we can neglect it badly, but it is still alive as long as we live. One of our great tasks is to liberate this child again, to encourage it to ask those deep questions children ask. Then we will look at everything through wondering eyes and receive everything with an open heart.

This awakening of the child within is not simpleminded sentimentality; it is at the heart of the monastic venture and of all spirituality. The real goal is what the philosopher Paul Ricoeur calls "second naiveté": to combine the fresh enthusiasm of the child's innocence with the wisdom that comes with experience.

If the morning light signals the gift of existence, the mystery of this gift transcends any response we can make. And that transcendence, that overabundance, is an essential ingredient in the divine gratuity that invites a fresh and wholehearted response each day and inspires the spontaneous praise that is chant.

Chant appeals to the child in us because it expresses pure delight in being alive. The praise of God that permeates even mournful melodies of chant is the expression of that delight. Joy is something we can cultivate: Once we begin to hear this thankful delight in chant, once its beauty captures our hearts, it is easy and natural to begin to practice gratefulness.

People associate monasticism and monks with asceticism, and that is correct. But they often think that asceticism means a denial of the senses, and there they go wrong. We've learned from traditions like Zen that asceticism means disciplining the senses so that you develop your capacity to experience every dimension of existence with heightened sensitivity. Monasticism at its best has emphasized this always and in all traditions. To the truly alert palate, a drink of spring water is full of flavor.

Rightly understood, asceticism means training. The word comes from the training of athletes, *askesis* in Greek. When we seek quality in our life, we study, we develop techniques, we refine our language, movements, and diet. So, too, with spirituality.

If, for example, you want to refine your diet, you might have to deny yourself things that you find tasty and quite enjoyable. But if you really care about your health, and work on improving your diet by cooking and eating what's good for you and tastes good as well, you quickly find that you haven't denied yourself anything you truly need. So it is with asceticism. The seasoned runner, the healthy gourmet, the virtuoso musician, the master gardener—anyone who hones a passion for excellence of some kind into a disciplined art—gladly forgoes some things to attain a refinement through discipline that brings immense vitality and joy.

In all our worldly busyness, there is a dulling of the senses. Our senses and awareness are so overloaded that they easily lose their acuity. Our eardrums are often so bombarded, our taste buds so overwhelmed, our diet so rich and overabundant, that we can't really hear anything well or savor what we eat.

Chant, with its lean lines of arresting simplicity, its transcendent beauty, asks for our full attention. Emerging from deep silence, it quiets the mind as we drink it in with our heart as much as with our ears. It is a kind of music that does not dull our hearing, but refines it. And its "ascetic" beauty, its disciplined but wholehearted presentation, effortlessly communicates the gift of disciplined life.

WHILE THE JOYOUS CHANT of Lauds praises God for a world reborn each morning, a world of delight and surprise, of refinement and celebration, we should not forget the other side to Lauds: When the cock crows, it's judgment hour. In the hymns for Lauds, the cock is called the messenger of light. But we are also reminded of Peter's betraying Jesus three times before the cock crows.

What has gone on in the dark, hidden part of our lives must be exposed to the light. This is a truly positive kind of judgment; not a condemnation, but a facing of reality when we are buoyed up by the thrill and promise of a new day. The sun judges the works of the darkness; they are brought to light. But this is the light of God's inexhaustible mercy. The very sound of the cock crowing conveys this special blending of joy and sadness, sobriety and enthusiasm. The rooster's cry is a sobbing, but it is a triumphant sobbing.

Weeping can be a triumph over anger: the melting of our inner frozenness. The blending of tears and joy gives a unique flavor to chant.

WHEN WE GREET the new day as a gift, a sense of gratefulness can carry us through the hours that follow. The day is presented to us as something to give away to others hour by hour. If we ask, for instance, at the beginning of the day, not "How can I get the most out of this day?" but "Whom can I make a little happier?" we ourselves will be much happier in the end. Someone who experiences the early morning sun as a gift is more likely to go around like a little sun shining on other people. We can smile. We can warm other people. We can brighten their day.

In almost every situation, we have a choice: We can be niggardly or generous. I've experienced that many times with regard to tipping. I've never regretted giving a little too big a tip, even if the service was less than great. Maybe it wasn't so great because the poor waiter or waitress needed a boost. I have always enjoyed the thought that a tip can light up someone else's day and maybe even turn it around.

Generosity can be contagious in a healthy way. The person who receives gets the message that this is not just a practical *quid pro quo* exchange ("I have strictly measured your performance, and this is your fair compensation"). Being generous creates an atmosphere that is more sacred, a sense that the world blesses us in unexpected ways, often in ways we obviously don't deserve. And that, of course, is the truth about our lives.

We can also be generous with our compassion. I have found that just lightly touching a person in a caring gesture sends a powerful message of kindness. Our world is so alienating, we are so literally out of touch with one another. Anything we do to communicate concretely that we really care about one another helps. It creates a sense of belonging, a sense that we are sisters and brothers in this home of ours, which is the whole world.

JESUS' SAYING "You are the light of the world" is often understood in too limited a sense. It means more than telling others about doctrine, no matter how enlightening the message may be. To me it means, "Listen, this is a dark world. If you shine, you light it up a little. You can make this world a little brighter. Shine!"

The monastic experience of greeting the sunrise with gratefulness is readily available. To watch the vast darkness of the night sky gradually dissipating and the sun come bursting forth over the horizon can seem amazing, miraculous. But for most of us this is a rare experience. Unless we are camping, or attending a sunrise Easter service, or dashing to catch an early plane, we tend to deny ourselves this daily miracle. Why miss this opportunity?

Even in the most artificial environment, there are many ways in which we can attune ourselves to the natural rhythms of the day. For monks, of course, this is not difficult. Everybody in a monastery gets up early. One can even get used to getting up early—and the joy of it is such an incentive! But I know ordinary people who heroically get up early enough to take a little time to meditate or pray just as dawn is about to break—before the children get up and all the noise starts—even if it's just a few minutes. Once we try it, we find that we get a great deal out of it. Often it is not even a matter of getting up earlier, just a matter of attentiveness.

If you are commuting and get onto the bus or into the car when it is still dark, stop thinking about the day ahead and just pay attention to the moment when light comes out of darkness: "I'm being given a new day." And with that, the angel of Lauds invites us to think: "What attitude should I bring to this day? What is it time for? Time to rise and shine."

PRIME
_
DELIBERATE BEGINNING

THE HYMN OF PRIME BEGINS WITH THE WORDS, "The sun has risen." The first two hours have been somewhat meditative. Now the stage is set for moving into action. Prime is the hour when work duties are given out. The focus is on a proper beginning. To start the day's activities properly, wholeheartedly.

Prime is centered in the chapter room, which is where the monks meet to address the practical concerns of the community. The work is given out in community. Even though we monks often work much of the day alone, it's common work.

Robert Frost expresses this beautifully when he claims that humans always work together, "whether they work together or apart." Frost speaks of a farm worker who goes out to turn the hay early in the morning. The one who had cut the grass had cut it much earlier in the morning and had left. So this man turning the hay feels alone, feels lonely there, and says to himself, "I must be, as he had been— alone. As all must be," he muses in his heart, "whether they work together or apart." But then a butterfly calls his attention to a tuft of flowers that this mower had left standing because they were too beautiful to cut down. The shared experience of the flowers' beauty moves him to change his mind: "And dreaming as it were [I] held brotherly speech with one whose thought I had not hoped to reach. 'Men work together,' I told him from the heart, 'whether they work together or apart.'" His sudden insight shows him that work is always community work, whether we realize it or not. All work intertwines.

This world was given to us to work on. Cultivating it we come to a deep understanding of the divine reality with which every part of creation is charged. Rilke says in one of his poems to God, "We grasp you only by acting." The German word for grasping means both holding something in your hands, seizing, and putting your hands into something, as you do when shaping clay. Only in this way do we grasp the divine reality.

Sometimes people have gotten the idea that we grasp the divine the more we separate ourselves from material reality. But creation spirituality rightly emphasizes that we discover the divine *in* the material. Just as the tuft of flowers was the point where the mower and the hay turner found contact, so material reality is our point of contact with the divine.

In the monastery, it is important to receive your work as a challenge rather than as just a routine chore. It is never the same work as yesterday: it's a new day, a new challenge, a new opportunity.

We learn in the monastery to savor our work as we are doing it—doing it for its own sake, not just doing it to have it done, or to get it over with. We need to resist our tendency to rush into things and to hurry through our activities. Our culture tells us that "time is money" and that work is a necessary evil, purely a means to an end. We want to get it over with. If we add up all the times we have spent in our life getting things over with, it may turn out to be half our lives. But the monastic attitude is to begin deliberately and to do anything we do with an even, stately pace and with wholehearted attention. This is how master artisans, weavers, experienced farmers, and other sage laborers work. That way even difficult tasks can be done leisurely and with joy, for their own sake. And then they become life-giving.

At Prime, the giving out of the work includes both blessing the work and distributing it. We pray that God may guide our actions. When we do our work in this way, then everything becomes prayer. This is not just some sort of pious and narrow religious notion. As Rilke says, "Basically, there are only prayers." Everything we do, in the sight of God, is prayer. In that way, our hands are hallowed, blessed. They cannot create anything that does not pray. "Whether one paints or mows," the poet continues, "already in the movement of the tools prayerfulness unfolds."

If you make the right start, aligning your actions with your best intentions, then everything you do is prayer. Prime is that hour of the day when we pray not to get it over with, but to make everything we do prayer.

All time management experts advise us to begin by planning our day. If you actually stop and take time to think ahead and plan, you'll get your priorities clear and work efficiently. During Prime, you can take the opportunity to examine your conscience ahead of time, and give some thought to what really matters. You set your priorities according to your heartfelt intentions. You can recall what your review of the day taught you at Compline last night, and how you can do better.

Monks take a vow of obedience. But obedience in the monastic context does not mean just doing what you are told, the sort of obedience a dog learns in obedience school.

It means a loving listening: listening to the Word of God that comes to us moment by moment, listening to the message of the angel that comes to us hour by hour.

The very word obedience means an intensive listening. The opposite of that obedience is absurdity, which means being deaf to life's challenges and meaning. We have the choice in our life between living with this loving listening or finding everything absurd. That absurdity is not outside of ourselves; it is in us. We are just deaf if we are not obedient listeners. So the next time you say, "This is absurd," you might consider the more helpful question, "To what am I deaf here?"

Disobedience is not so much not doing what you know you should do, as not even listening to what the situation demands and calls you to do. Rigid obedience can be a not listening. Just following the rules doesn't deserve the name of true obedience. There is a message in everything that happens, in every situation in which we find ourselves, whether we like it or not. If we make the right response, it will be life-affirming and life-giving for us and for others. It's in those moments that our character is decided. That's when morality really happens. With every moment we have a choice: to respond wholeheartedly, authentically, or to wimp out and betray our true self.

It's very painful to see how small betrayals can gradually eat away at our soul. We see people who haven't made any big mistakes in their lives, perhaps just a recurrent stubbornness, little mistakes that they insist on making over and over again. But their lives end up a horrendous mess, just as bad as if they had committed one enormously harmful deed. Our little infidelities, our little moments of giving in to our whims or lazy habits, are cumulative and can do more harm than we think. It's not only a moral concern; the very joy of life hinges on it. When we are sloppy with our moments, hastily diving into our actions or words without any forethought, we create a lot of wasted moments.

And yet, no matter what we've gotten into, this very moment can be the beginning of a new life. God has forgiven us before we ever failed. We need only accept this forgiveness and forgive ourselves to make a brand-new start. So beginning the work day with conscious clarity and high intention is vital to the quality of our lives.

THE ANGEL OF PRIME has the brightest face of all because it reflects the sun. This angel is playing the drum, getting us ready, just as in the circus somebody beats the drum for the acrobat to leap or the lion to jump through the hoop. Prime is the drum roll for the day.

DURING PRIME, we commit ourselves to do everything today in the same way that we teach children to cross a street: stop, look, then go. To start the day off right, the first step is to stop. It is so easy to plunge immediately into the middle of whatever you want to do without having deliberately started. Starting deliberately requires beginning with a pause, even if it is just a fraction of a second. Without it, we just get swept along, as happens all too often.

This deliberate starting is expressed in chant, in which everything depends on coming in at the right moment. To come in at the right moment, we must first pause.

When the conductor lifts the baton, the whole orchestra is silent for a moment—*then* it starts on the downbeat. If the conductor just went directly to the podium and immediately started waving his baton, there'd never be music, just a chaos of sound. That moment of silence before the music starts is vital also when we chant.

The second element is to look. It doesn't help you to stop if you don't look. The choir has to look at the cantor, at his gesture, for the start. When you do anything, it's important first to look at all that concerns this action—how you did it when you did it before, what you did well and what you did not so well—and not to make the same mistake too often.

As they say, a fool makes the same mistake over and over again, a wise person makes a new mistake every time. We can't avoid making mistakes, but at least we can avoid the ones we have already made. Unfortunately, we tend to avoid assiduously looking at what we don't like to see. But honest looking can be learned.

Finally, we must go. It doesn't help us to stop if we don't look, and it doesn't help us to stop and look if we don't go. We must at last act. All three belong together, and this drum roll of the angel signals, "Stop, look, go! Let's get the show on the road."

To bring the spirit of Prime into everyday life, we stop and remember that whatever we are doing is a contribution to what we all do, if it is at all worth doing. Of course, there's work that isn't. But if it is at all worth doing, even if you are just doing one little thing on a conveyor belt, one could keep in mind that this helps the whole human enterprise, that we all are working together with others whom we will never see.

That idea connects again with chant, where you are singing together with others. That's part of what makes the chant so beautiful: It is not just one voice singing, but it is the community singing. And it is not only the community singing, but quite consciously singing with all of creation, with the birds, with the waves, and with the angels, with visible and invisible creation.

Work, if we don't approach it consciously, will suck us into its demands. Then we become slaves, no matter how high up we are on the ladder. It is only by beginning deliberately, learning to "Stop, look, go," that we can remain masters of the work, taking it up deliberately as the moment requires. One of the reasons why monks drop everything when the bell rings is precisely to prove to themselves that they are not under the law of work, but that they are free to let it go when the time comes.

If we are not intentional and mindful in our work, then we are slaves to it and end up feeling alienated and empty. Even people who have to do jobs they don't like and find meaningless can still be free within them, at least to a certain extent, by reminding themselves, deliberately and often, why they do them. As long as we do our work out of love for those whom we love, we do it for a good reason. Love is the best reason for our labors. Love makes what we do and suffer rise like music, like a soaring line of chant.

TERCE

—

BLESSING

TERCE CELEBRATES THE THIRD HOUR OF THE DAY. It comes in the middle of the morning and is one of the so-called little hours, the upbeat mid-morning hour. Somewhat irreverently, we might call it a monastic coffee break, a little prayer break. But its brief duration does not mean that it is of small significance.

By this time of the day, you've been working or studying for several hours. Even though work assignments have been given out at Prime, the earlier morning is often study time in monasteries, except when there is much outdoors work in summer.

Now, at the third hour of the day, the focus of prayer is on the Holy Spirit. The Spirit is called down on all our work, especially in the text of the hymn we chant at this hour. For Terce reminds us of the outpouring of the Holy Spirit at Pentecost. Those who ran together as the Spirit descended like a mighty storm and flames of fire were amazed. Others accused the apostles, who were talking in different languages, of being drunk. Filled with the Spirit, Peter jovially replied, "We are not drunk; after all, it is only the third hour [that is, it's only the middle of the morning]."

One of the hymns speaks of the "sober inebriation" enjoyed by those filled with the Holy Spirit.

We experience the outpouring of God's Holy Spirit in blessing. Blessing is that Spirit, that life-breath, that aliveness, that we celebrate at this hour. The morning is still fresh, our energy is at its peak, we feel bursting with vitality and the joy of living. This is the time to appreciate the life pulsing in our veins and to realize that our aliveness is the divine life-breath within us. We all are Adam—"earthlings"—into whose nostrils God blows the divine life-breath. Genesis says, "And so Adam became a living creature." The physical, mental, and spiritual dimensions of life, though distinct, cannot be separated.

We "live and breathe and have our being" by sharing in God's life. Ultimately, life is the primal energy that fuels the universe. That aliveness flows into us as blessing and wants to flow out from us as blessing to others. We can bless others with a good word or a smile, a kind action that goes completely unobserved, or simply a good wish in silence. What joy to become aware of blessing, of that special aliveness flowing into us and through us.

The original blessing is life, is breath, is spirit. And for us humans, that always means more than mere vitality. It means a super-aliveness, a divine vitality infinitely more intense than the natural life that we see all around us. Our participation in the now that is not subject to time implies this timeless, eternal life in us. We must not take this blessing for granted. Everything depends on becoming aware of it and passing it on.

One traditional image of the Holy Spirit is the mighty wind, air, the breath of life. Another image is water, a fountain, a great river. The river Jordan is the great source of blessing for the Holy Land. It's the life source for Palestine, for Israel. This river of blessing flows into the lake of Galilee, and anyone who has ever visited there, at any time of year, will remember the banks of that lake as a paradise. Then the Jordan flows out of that lake and on, and eventually empties into the Dead Sea. But this body of water is absolutely dead. No fish can live in it. Its shores are parched desert. The difference between these two bodies of water is that the Jordan flows into the lake of Galilee and then out again: The blessing flows in and the blessing flows out. In the Dead Sea, it only flows in and stays there. All day long, we receive blessing after blessing. Will we pass these blessings on? Sharing or deadness, paradise or desert: We have the choice.

To be conscious of the myriad blessings in our life is to be like a rich person who can be generous without fear of ever running out of resources. We can practice, if only for a few moments, paying attention to our breathing: Each breath flows in as a blessing; each breath flows out as a sharing of that blessing.

Blessing is well-wishing. We know that even plants we wish well grow better. Sick people for whom we pray and send good thoughts have a better chance of getting well. Even scholarly research proves this. Prayer does indeed have healing effects. Most of all, prayer heals those who pray. When asked if he thought prayer changed God, C.S. Lewis observed, "Prayer doesn't change God, it changes me." In changing me, prayer changes the world, for everything hangs together with everything else.

I always associate Terce with the monastery kitchen, because the day's main meal, the noonday meal, is prepared in the morning. Around this time there is always somebody in the kitchen, and you hear all the sweet kitchen noises: the chopping of carrots on the board, the clanking of ladles and pots, the gushing of water into the kitchen sink. The food and its preparation, the earth's constant bounty and the service of our fellow monks, are an elemental part of the sense of blessing that fills the spirit of this hour. St. Benedict says, "In the monastery, every pot and pan should be as sacred as the sacred vessels of the altar."

The monastic kitchen is an extremely important place. The monks in charge of the kitchen are always specially honored. That's true in the Buddhist tradition as well as the Christian. Food is a blessing, and cooks are channelers of this blessing. They receive a special benediction by the whole community as they start their duties for the week. And, of course, everyone takes a turn at cooking in the monastery. Not everybody is what we call "first kitchener" (I never made it to first kitchener), but everybody helps in some way: chopping, cleaning up, and so forth. And the whole process of tending the gardens, the harvesting, the cooking, connects us with the earth and each other, the essential blessings God gives us each day.

PEOPLE OFTEN IMAGINE monks eating gruel, but monasteries are renowned for their cheese, bread, beer, fruit-cakes, and other fine foods. The monastic idea is that even bread and water should be wholesome bread and pure water. We honor God by honoring God's gifts, by cultivating and refining what we're given and passing it on to others.

In the monastery, everything in space and time is so arranged that it fosters mindfulness, and cooking and eating with awareness and a sense of blessing is a vital way to make that mindfulness part of our everyday reality. Our brothers in Buddhist monasteries chant: "Seventy-two labors were necessary to bring us this food; we should know how it comes to us." Then Buddhists say, "Let us consider whether our virtue and practice deserve this food." We eat so as to be able to serve; we nourish ourselves to be of service to others and pass on in some form what we have received.

Realizing the blessing of aliveness expresses itself in humble, down-to-earth ways of service and taking care of details. And that is something that we can practice in any walk of life. It works both ways. As we lovingly take care of details, which so easily slip our mind as we focus on the seemingly big things, we grow into that attitude of caring and of tenderness. We have to cook and clean anyway, so we might as well do it lovingly and caringly.

In the hymn of Terce, we line up all our organs of praise: "My mouth, my tongue, my mind, my senses, my vitality, all should sound together in blessing God."

Sometimes people get the mistaken notion that spirituality is a separate department of life, the penthouse of our existence. But rightly understood, it is a vital awareness that pervades all realms of our being. Someone will say, "I come alive when I listen to music," or "I come to life when I garden," or "I come alive when I play golf." Wherever we come alive, that is the area in which we are spiritual. And then we can say, "I know at least how one is spiritual in that area." To be vital, awake, aware, in all areas of our lives, is the task that is never accomplished, but it remains the goal. Since we all know what it means to be alive in at least one area, we have some sense of what it must mean to be ablaze with the Holy Spirit in all of one's life.

THE ANGEL OF TERCE plays a dance instrument, expressing the delight in being blessed with life. The expression on all of Fra Angelico's angels is serene, but this one seems to smile with joyful exuberance. As with the other angels, the look is more inward than outward. It signals a rootedness in the deeper reality that is the true mindfulness we seek to cultivate. There is also a sweetness to the angel's gaze; this is a sweet hour, a tender hour. This angel, like all the angels depicted, has a flame on its head to symbolize the Holy Spirit's presence, both powerful and tender, incendiary and warming.

Both vivacity and delicacy belong to this hour of the Spirit. It is a time to enthusiastically celebrate the thrill of life and to exhibit tender caring. Blessing involves both a connection with the immensity of infinite spirit and a feeling of the intimate touch of God's love. The Spirit is energy and caring. So you can feel totally alive and exhilarated in a wild thunderstorm, but you can also be fully alive when a baby smiles.

The spirit in us is our strength. That strength expresses itself in strong action, but it also expresses itself in tenderness. Only when you are strong can you really be tender; otherwise, it's just weakness or sentimentality.

The angel of Terce is the messenger who calls us to enthusiasm, in the literal sense of being full of god, being inspired. Imbibing that enthusiasm in the spirited chant of

Terce and in a brief meditation on the blessing of being alive, and then sharing it with others, can bring fresh vitality and warmth to the day.

At Terce we pray that this fire of the Holy Spirit, this life-breath of the Holy Spirit, may set our heart aflame. We pray that this fire may also be spread in the world in the sense of Jesus' words, "I've come to cast fire on the world, and how I wish that it may blaze." It is the time to spread the fiery enthusiasm of the divine life within us throughout the worlds we live in.

It is easy to cast a jaundiced eye at happily pious people who are always saying "Thanks be to God" and "God be willing" and "Blessed be" this and that. But they often can have a simple but intense sense that life is a gift, and that they are part of a divinely charged world. Many of us know that it is the simple faithful—and not the sophisticated—who have the deepest spirituality.

Our feeling of being ill at ease in the world, which I spoke of earlier, signals our longing to share in that flow of blessing, to experience God's spirit in true enthusiasm, to feel that *joie de vivre* that is not just a passing mood. Chant is the music that expresses our connection to the whole. It tells

us that ultimately, we are not orphaned, we are not alienated. We have the spirit of the universe flowing through our
body. It flows as song out our mouths.

IN ANY WALK OF LIFE, you can build into your day
prayer breaks that connect you with the Spirit. They don't
have to be ten minutes long; they may be only ten seconds
long, yet they'll be helpful. I once knew two sisters who had
a clock that struck every fifteen minutes. With each strike of
the clock, one would say, "Remember God's presence" and
the other would add, "Let us always be grateful." It's such a
simple thing, a couple of times a day or every hour on the
hour, to remember we stand in God's presence. St. Benedict
stresses this as the essence of prayer. That's why I have a
clock that chimes every hour—it's my portable monastery,
which I can take with me wherever I go.

The inner gesture of Terce, which is available to all of
us at any time, is to simply stop for a few moments and open
yourself to the force of love that drives the universe. Stop
and bless. Stop and appreciate. Take note of the gifts of
your life and share them.

SEXT

—

FERVOR
AND
COMMITMENT

SEXT IS THE HOUR OF FERVOR AND COMMITMENT, but it is also the hour of temptation to laziness and despair: the hour of the noonday devil as well as the angel of intensity. Sext comes right in the middle of the day, in the middle of everything. It is the middle of our life each day, the time of opportunity and the time of crisis.

At high noon, the sun stands at its apex. But although this is the time of the full blazing of the sun, like a blaring trumpet, it is also a time of great silence. Even the birds are silent; often, you only hear the buzzing of the bees and the drone of the flies. At this turning point in time we decide the fate of our day, and cumulatively the fate of our lives. Do we renew our fervor and commitment, or do we let the forces of entropy drain our resolve?

The Angelus bells are also connected with noon. The bells ring when the day has reached its peak, and at that point we pray the Angelus. The Angelus prayer, whose name comes from the opening word of the Annunciation story in the Gospel ("The angel announced unto Mary . . . ") and recounts the angel telling Mary that she would be the mother of the son of God, celebrates the breaking of eternity into time. And that is really what every angel announces: the eternal now breaking into our time.

Stopping at high noon for a moment of reflection is a spontaneous gesture of human consciousness. I remember when Tetsugen Glassman Sensei was being ordained the Abbot of Riverside Zendo in New York. It was a grand affair. Zen teachers from all over the country were gathered together to celebrate the event, with candles and incense and white chrysanthemums and black and gold brocade garments. In the middle of this solemn celebration, the beeper on somebody's wristwatch suddenly went off. Everybody was surreptitiously looking around to find the poor guy to whom this had happened, because generally you are not even supposed to wear a wristwatch in the Zendo. To everybody's surprise, the new Abbot himself interrupted the ceremony and said, "This was my wristwatch, and it was not a mistake. I have made a vow that regardless of what I am doing, I will interrupt it at noon and will think thoughts of peace." And then he invited everyone there to think thoughts of peace for a world that needs it.

That incident reminded me that the Angelus bells were really instituted in the first place to announce a prayer for peace. They were the bells for Sext in the monastery, but they invited everyone in the village to pray for peace. Wherever people were, in the fields or at their labors, in their shops or at home, when they heard the Angelus bells they would stop work and pray. That was also true with the morning bells and with the evening bells, but the noon bells were especially an invitation to pray for peace and to commit oneself to treat others with love.

I have told the story of the Abbot's installation many times, and I always find that people are eager to help revive this custom. Now, all over the world, people are praying at high noon for peace, as we have done in the monastery for hundreds of years. How beautiful it would be to hear bells and gongs from famous shrines ring out peace on radio and television at high noon.

IN MONASTERIES THAT HAVE only one common meal, the main meal is at noon. A common meal in a monastery is always a celebration. And even hermits, who live on their own outside the monastery, are strongly encouraged to eat their meals with care and awareness: "Don't just grab something to eat," we're advised, "set the table, put some flowers and maybe a candle on it, and celebrate your meal, even if it's very simple."

Even though you may be eating all by yourself, you are in communion with all. Eating is always a communion, a celebration with all those who have labored to bring you this food, with all those creatures who have lived and died to give you this food, and with all others who eat on earth. It's a symbolic participation in the wedding feast that is already the wedding feast of eternity. So for the noon meal in the monastery, the monks usually file in solemnly from chanting the Sext office. Sometimes, on the way, they recite a psalm; and then before sitting down to eat, they say a prayer of thanksgiving over the food. Usually, the monks eat in silence, as one of them reads to the others from a worthwhile book. This wonderful custom is still practiced in many monasteries today, and many books are read in common in the community.

Inseparable from Sext in the monastery is the practice of serving one another at mealtime. There are always servers at table who bring the food, and the monks themselves are encouraged by the rule of St. Benedict not to ask for anything they need, but always to look out for what a neighbor needs. (There's a famous story of a monk who notices as he is eating his soup that a mouse has dropped into his bowl. What is he to do? He is to pay attention to his neighbors' needs, not his own. So he helps himself by calling the server and pointing out, "My neighbor hasn't got a mouse.")

The servers rotate weekly and are strengthened by the special blessing they receive at Sext on Sunday before and after their week of service. Everyone, including the Abbot, serves. On Holy Thursday, when Jesus himself served his disciples, the Abbot washes the feet of the monks. That is usually done in the church in connection with Maundy Thursday services, but it's also done in some monasteries in the refectory. Maundy Thursday received its name from the "mandate" Jesus Christ gave to his followers on this day, when he said, "I am among you as the one who serves." So the greatest among you should be the servant of all. The idea of service is prominent in every eating ritual.

THE NOONDAY ANGEL is the only one shown in full profile here. It's the time of transition, passing into the second part of the day. The angel is blowing the trumpet with full force, cheeks swelled out. The hour is rousing us to summon the courage to stay the course, to remain true to our ideals through the rest of the day.

The hour, as we may waver, lose our resolve at midday, shouts to us the message of God's unstinting love. To our worrying, midday questions—"Am I alone?" "Is the universe arbitrary, uncaring?" "What's the point?"—we receive the forceful answer that the ultimate reality in which we are immersed cares for us like a parent or like a lover.

The answer to the existential question, "Who am I?" is quintessentially, "I am loved."

Prayer is not sending in an order and expecting it to be fulfilled. Prayer is attuning yourself to the life of the world, to love, the force that moves the sun and the moon and the stars. We can close our hearts to that Tao of the universe, and because we so often do, alienation and lack of peace tear the world apart. But to the extent that we attune ourselves to the flow of life, to our life breath, our lives can become peaceful even in an alienated and torn world. To that extent, the world also becomes more peaceful. God works with us and in us. Also, as I noted before, it's not what our prayers do to God, but how we ourselves are changed by encountering God in prayer.

The power that God wields is the power of love, and that is a most vulnerable power. Paradoxically, it's really the power of weakness. You can actually hear that power in the chant. It's not a power of overpowering might, but of truth, and that's a highly vulnerable power.

Praying for peace entails believing that peace begins with you, and aligning yourself with peacefulness. Peace is understood in the Christian tradition as *tranquillitas ordinis,* the quietness of order, the calm that comes with harmony. And order is arranging things so that each gives to the other its proper place. Even God must do this. In the Jewish tradition it is said that, in order to create the world, God had to step back.

There is also an urgency to prayer, a fervor. For it is at its heart the expression of love, a sharing of feelings of joy, appreciation, admiration. In the last analysis, wherever there is love, there is only prayer. When our heart is in the right place and brimming with love, everything becomes prayer.

SEXT IS ASSOCIATED with the stillness and peace of noon, but it also evokes crisis and danger. Crisis is always a purification if we understand it correctly. The very word "crisis" comes from a root that means sifting out. Crisis is a separation, a sifting out of that which is viable and can go on from that which is dead and has to be left behind.

Personal crisis always has three elements. First, you feel that you can't go on like this, that you're up against a wall. Then you feel that something has to be sloughed off if you are to go on. The third and most important element in that process is guidance. We need guidance; otherwise, we do not know what to slough off and how to get to the other side of this apparently impenetrable wall. That guidance is what I have called the life force or blessing. If we come up against the wall and we open ourselves to ask, "What can guide me now? I am helpless, but I trust that there is some guidance," we will always receive an answer. Sometimes this guidance will come to us unexpectedly: We read some-thing that seems to speak directly to our situation, or we meet a person who says just the right thing. But sometimes the realignment will be completely internal: a dream, an unbidden insight, a serendipitous event. And all of a sudden the guidance we need is there. What we have to bring to the crisis is trust. And trustful waiting is a truly fervent way of praying.

An essential message of Sext is to deal with crises, to face challenges one step at a time. Sext represents a time when our good intentions, our enthusiasm, can begin to flag. All of us have our own version of the noonday devil. Jewish tradition teaches that even when you don't feel like doing what you're supposed to do, just do it. Say the prayer, perform the mitzvah. In time, your feelings will catch up with your doing. We know, for instance, that when we fall into depression, of which the noonday devil is an archetypal symbol, what really helps is to keep moving: just keep on doing what you should be doing, whether you like it or not, whether you feel like it or not.

The noonday devil is the voice of negativity and despair and sadness. Its opposite, its opposing angel, is joy. The sadness that is the true opposite of joyfulness is not being disheartened that something has happened; it is the feeling of not rising to the occasion, not making the effort to meet the invitation of the moment.

Chant reminds us that sorrow—distress at some calamity, a child's death, a friendship lost, a major disappointment—is compatible with joy. Chant can be quite sorrowful in the midst of its joy, but it is never sad. It embraces the vicissitudes of life—a lot of chanting is singing the psalms—without succumbing to dejection, because it is grounded in fervently committed faith.

NONE

—

shadows GROW LONGER

NONE IS THE HOUR OF MID- TO LATE AFTERNOON, as the day begins to decline and shadows begin to lengthen. It is natural to feel some anxiety as the day wanes and to seek God's strength as the light begins to fade.

We have been following the waxing and now waning of the light through the rhythm of the hours. The day begins in darkness, then the light breaks through, it reaches its peak at noon, and now we are in the descending half. It is a time to begin to face decline, disappointment, the little death of each passing day.

The chant associated with None, while it is not that different from the chant heard during the other hours, has a strain of serenity at this time, when "day declines and evening shadows fall," as the hymns for this hour puts it.

Earlier in the day, vigor and enthusiasm held sway, but with None we encounter the reality that in human life things don't last forever. How do we deal with the fact that we can't keep something forever? How to deal with the inescapable impermanence of life is precisely the question of this hour.

The fading of time, the passing of everything, is brought home to us as we see the shadows lengthen. "Be near us with your light that never fades," we sing and turn to the One who remains "unchanged, while endless ages run."

This angel's message is that death and impermanence are part of life. And we need to connect with something transcendent, beyond time, because the temporal things are going to fade. Now, when the things we might have relied on in the course of the day give out on us and are seen to be transitory, we look to those things which endure.

Chant embodies both impermanence and endurance. Not one note lasts more than a second or so. Chant is movement and change. And yet the continuum of chanting through all rhythmic and melodic changes conveys a quality of permanence and timelessness.

THE SPACE IN THE MONASTERY associated with None is the monk's cell. There are many sayings of the Fathers about the cell being your paradise, your place of peace. But the cell is also the place where you have to be alone with yourself, where you have to face yourself. The sheltering presence of God is reinforced through the chanting, prayers, and meditation throughout the day, but still you have to face yourself, confront your shortcomings, and forgive yourself and others in light of God's limitless forgiveness. The monastic cell is a place of forgiveness. It's a place to face reality and to make peace.

In a sense, home in the monastery is ultimately one's cell, the inescapable symbol of the truth that we are, in a very real way, "alone with the Alone." The simple cell for just one person tells us that we each stand before God alone. Deep in our heart we are alone with the Alone. Mysteriously, the word "alone" can be read as "all one." When we face our aloneness, when we enter our heart of hearts and confront God, we are united with all, just as the individual cells are all clustered in a single monastery.

The aloneness of the cell, of course, also suggests the aloneness of death. In that mid-afternoon hour, when the shadows lengthen, we remember death. We actually pray at this hour every day for a holy death, for a peaceful death, for a death that will complete our lives. For many people today, this is an important concern: a death with dignity, a death that brings our life full circle and makes it a completed whole rather than just an unraveling.

We fear death most when we feel that we haven't lived yet. We're frightened that death will come like a thief in the night before we've really had a chance to live. This fear is most real when we are not living in the moment. If we don't find ways to live in the now, then death is frightening because we've never really been present to our life. We missed it and now, all of a sudden, it's over.

The more fully we live, the easier it is to let go, to die. Monks are taught to have death at all times before their eyes. Remembering death does not mean being preoccupied with death. It means that you are preoccupied with life because you know this is now your opportunity. Carlos Casteneda relates in one of his books that Don Juan said to him, "You are so moody, and you are not really full of life, because you don't have death as your adviser. You think that you will live forever."

To acknowledge that each day comes to a close, that each life comes to a close, is to hear the challenge to rise to the occasion and make something of this day, this life. When you make something of the day, you will also be able to let go. The more we give ourselves to the enjoyment of a vacation or a weekend in a beautiful place, the more we will be ready, when it is time, to leave it behind and give ourselves also to our everyday life refreshed.

The contemporary theologian John Dunne sees the choices we make in shaping our lives as so many answers to the problem of death. He phrases it this way: "Given the fact that we have to die, how do we satisfy our desire to live?" The monastic way is one way of satisfying that desire to live so that you will have lived the moments of your days. Whenever we remember our mortality, there's a better chance that we will do the things that make us truly happy and fulfilled.

Everyone can have this sobering yet invigorating experience of facing the waning of each day, of facing the fact that our days are numbered. Some people create spaces in their homes—an altar, a meditation closet—where they can see their day and their lives in a larger context. We all need a cell, a place apart, to face reality.

THE ANGEL OF THIS HOUR has a faint purple gown and dark wings, reflecting the sweet melancholy of this time of day, and almost seems to be muffling the sound of the tambourine after playing it vigorously. This angel again has an inward look that reminds us that None is the time to turn inward again. After the outward movement of the day and all its activities, the day curves back in on itself, as the angel's hand gently stills the sound of his instrument. Yet, in stopping the tambourine, stopping the sound of the music and of the dance, this angel of None is listening intently to the music that never stops, to that inner music, the music of silence.

THE VIRTUE OF NONE is forgiveness. "At evening God draws everything home." It is the time when we are forgiven our shortcomings and are encouraged to forgive ourselves and others.

There are different forms of giving appropriate to the different hours of the day. First, there is giving up, in the sense of offering up the work of our hands. This is an obviously life-giving form of giving: Giving up always goes together with keeping up, holding up our end of the bargain, fulfilling our obligations. That's what we have committed ourselves to at Prime: this taking care that goes with giving up.

Taking possession is the opposite of giving up. Taking possession is literally a sitting on, a stifling; if you sit on something long enough, it dies. The giving up and keeping up, on the other hand, is the kind of gesture a parent makes all life long: at first, physically, to give the child up to give it life, but then, step by step, giving the child up in the course of the child's life.

A second form of giving, which we can practice all day long, is giving thanks. It, too, goes together with taking, because give and take always go together. So the giving thanks goes together with taking to heart. You cannot really give thanks for something you have not taken to heart. I have spoken earlier about this taking to heart when I talked about openness, receptivity, mindfulness, aliveness. When you are dull and take things for granted, that's the opposite of giving thanks.

And now comes the third and greatest form of giving, at the end of the day—forgiving. Forgiving is over against taking offense. Of course, compared with taking possession and taking for granted, taking offense is the most stupid of all "takings," because we are taking something we don't even want. Forgiving is also the greatest of all giving. It is so difficult for us, because it involves taking the blame. Not in a legalistic sense—"I might have done it," "There but for the grace of God go I"—but in the sense that when you really forgive, you forgive from your heart of hearts. And in that heart of hearts you are one with all, and also one with whomever you have a grievance. There's no one to blame. You are taking *away* the blame by forgiving.

"Forgive us as we forgive," we ask. Jesus says, "Those to whom you forgive their offenses, these offenses will be forgiven." When you forgive, God forgives. In fact, God has forgiven "before always"; we are invited to let God's forgiveness flow through us into the world. The offenses are simply gone, wiped out. This biblical tradition seems a different notion from the law of karma, that inexorable law of having to make up for everything that you have done wrong. But the deeper understanding of karma, say in the Buddhist tradition, is that compassion is our true vocation and compassion yields forgiveness. Ultimately, compassion dispels karma and frees us from the cycle of attachment and suffering. This is a profound point where the Christian and the Buddhist traditions actually meet. But it isn't often seen that clearly, either by Buddhists or by Christians.

It is true that the cumulative character you develop as you respond or fail to respond to the challenges of the moment constitutes a kind of karmic self, the state of our soul. But this rather grim reality needs as its counterpoint the insight that even whatever karma has accumulated can all be dissolved by heartfelt, compassionate forgiveness. If something remains to be worked out in practical reality, the sting is taken out of it. It's no longer destructive and life-denying. Suffering that yields compassion is creative and life-affirming.

The late afternoon of our lives is often a time when we are called to forgive. If we respond to the angel of this hour and let go of all that we are holding against anyone, the evening of our life will be clear.

AS THE SHADOWS LENGTHEN, we have intimations of the end of the day. We notice the limits and boundaries that give our lives structure. The hour of None wants to lead us to the right understanding of limits: to see them not as prisons, but to face them and work within them. And if they are arbitrary limits that inhibit our genuine growth, then we must overcome them.

Our lives have many structures—our jobs, our families—because it's only within limits that anything meaningful can happen. If all possibilities were available at all moments, if there were no limits, no boundaries, no definitions, we'd be lost. People mistakenly think that happiness comes from removing all limits. The lesson of the lengthening shadows is to forgive and to live to the full within the inherent limits and boundaries of our lives.

VESPERS
-
LIGHTING
THE LAMPS

VESPERS CELEBRATES THE LIGHTING OF THE lamps as evening descends. It is a counterpart to Lauds, in which we celebrated the coming of the natural light.

At Vespers you've put your tools away, taken off your apron, your work clothes, washed up, and put on your robes again. Now you come freshly dressed for the solemn evening celebration at sunset, when darkness descends and the monastery is lit with lamps and candles. It is the hour of peace of heart, of serenity.

The time just after sunset has a magical quality. In the evening light, trees, figures, even faces, are "silhouetted against the dim sky," as T. S. Eliot saw it. The world seems perfectly framed, intensely beautiful. Sometimes, after the sun has set, the clouds begin to glow with colors of water and colors of fire. Buildings and mountains also glow, and the sun is reflected like molten gold in the windows of far-away houses. It is a wonderful time to take a walk, as monks often do after dinner and, of course, on the way to the oratory to sing Vespers.

The monastery garden is the place I associate with Vespers. Usually, a monastery is built in a square with a garden in the center. Often, a covered cloister walk surrounds a grassy enclosure, with a fountain in the center and a trim herb and flower garden around it. The monks call that enclosure with the fountain paradise, given its simple, tranquil perfection, its delicious fragrances, its multicolored blooms in summer, and its coating of pure white snow in winter. Placing a garden in the center of the monastery conveys the centrality of nature and her rhythms in monastic life. The garden teaches us each day that life is a round of gestation, birth, growth, flowering, fruitbearing, fading, dying, and new gestation in the dark of winter.

At eventide, the daylight fades and the distinct silence of night descends. The only sounds are those of nature—crickets and frogs—and little white moths fly up from the grass.

THE ANGEL OF VESPERS, in the evening blue robe, has stopped playing and serenely holds the tambourine with the evening star on it. The angel reminds me of T. S. Eliot's lines from the last of the *Choruses from the Rock:* "In our rhythm of earthly life we tire of light. We are glad when the day ends, when the play ends . . . the day is long for work or play."

VESPERS IS THE HOUR that invites peace of heart, which is the reconciling of contradictions within ourselves and around us. Rilke has a beautiful poem in *The Book of Hours* in which he speaks of someone who makes peace among his life's many contradictions. It defies translation, but I will paraphrase it here.

> Whoever gathers his life's many contradictions into one, gratefully makes of them a single symbol, expels all the noisy ones from his palace and becomes in a new way festive. Then you, God, are the guest whom he receives in gentle evening hours. You are the second to his solitude, the quiet center of his monologues, and every time he circles around you, you stretch his compass beyond time.

Within time, again, we receive that which goes beyond time. Within this evening hour, when we become festive in a new way and receive God as a guest, we stretch that compass of time beyond time and embrace the now. That's the serenity, the peace of heart, the ability to embrace the inevitable contradictions the day leaves behind, which is the mood of Vespers.

When evening arrives—no matter what happened during the day, whatever *sturm und drang* occurred, whatever challenges were unmet, whatever disappointments and regrets—people have a universal desire to find a serene place where they can put all the parts of the day together in some tranquil way. Given the spirit of forgiveness of the prior hour, at Vespers we are free to let go of the day and to luxuriate in the quiet beauty of the evening.

The serenity of Vespers, wherein we gather together all the day's contradictions, is truly healing, since healing essentially involves a knitting together of what is apart, what is broken.

In J. S. Bach's St. Matthew's Passion, there's a beautiful passage: "In the evening when it was cool." In it, Bach recounts the various biblical events that happened in the cool of the evening. It was then that God walked with Adam and Eve in the Garden of Eden. In the evening, the dove came back to the ark of Noah, bringing the olive twig of peace in its beak. In the evening, Jesus is put into the grave, like a seed, to be reborn in the resurrection. Bach captures the consoling spirit of this blessed hour, which is also beautifully conveyed in the chanting of Vespers.

The high point of Vespers is the singing of the Magnificat, the song in the Gospel of Luke that Mary sings as she greets her cousin Elizabeth. "My soul proclaims the greatness of the Lord and my spirit exults in God my Savior. . . . " That song, praising God for our salvation, our ultimate reconciliation, is chanted every day of the year at Vespers. The evening office sees in the motherly image of Mary the maternal dimension of God as the one who loves us unconditionally, like a mother. The singing of the Magnificat at Vespers parallels the singing at Lauds of the hymn of Zacharias, which occurs in the same chapter of Luke. Zacharias declares, "Blessed be the Lord . . . for he has visited his people, he has come to their rescue."

These two great hymns are the pillars of the morning and the evening that support the day, and both celebrate our redemption. Redemption, at root, is the healing of the rift that runs through the world, the rift that we experience as alienation from ourselves and others and from the ground of our being, and for which we intuitively feel chant to be an antidote.

Even listening to chant is reconciling. Music of many kinds can be soothing and transforming. Chant, which springs from such deep prayerfulness, is especially powerful. We are never free of conflicts and contradictions, but praying and chanting together has a healing effect.

As you chant in community through the eight hours, day in and day out, its rhythmic tranquility becomes embedded in your soul. You carry it with you all the time, wherever you go. It creates an interior monastery. And it may well be that those of us who have chosen to live alone as hermits can do so only because we have first lived and chanted in community for years. Even your listening to chant at home will allow you to imbibe its monastic spirit and to make its sacred tranquility an integral dimension of your inner life. You might even gradually learn to sing along, using the words from the liner notes of the album. Maybe the monks of Santo Domingo de Silos can teach the world to chant; it would certainly make it a better place.

THE WAY THAT WE can actively bring the spirit of Vespers into everyday life is to light whatever lights we can in this dark world. As the Paulist motto has it, "It is better to light a candle than to curse the darkness." What candles can we light? A smile, a kind word, a visit?

Our society prizes rugged self-sufficiency, being able to handle things on our own. But this individualism yields so much loneliness and despair. It is remarkable how much people simply want to be acknowledged, to be seen, to be appreciated. We pretend that we don't need others to take us into account and to care for us. But as soon as someone shines the light of caring attention on us, our stoic facade melts.

We move closer together when it gets dark. The hour of Vespers is a call to neighborliness. We all need to move closer to our neighbors in this dark hour of history. If the community singing that informs chant can promote an enhanced sense of common caring in its listeners, then it will be a great monastic gift to the world.

COMPLINE
—
COMPLETING
THE CIRCLE

COMPLINE IS THE CONCLUSION OF THE monastic day. Entering the fullness of night, we return from song back into the silence that is the dark soil in which the flower of chant is rooted. In Compline we close the day, starting with a confession of our failings before the whole community. We examine our conscience and ask forgiveness, and thereby make a clean transition into night and sleep.

Compline means completion. It is the hour that completes the circle of the day. The chanting of the day is actually completed at Vespers, but Compline was added by the monks as a night prayer to bring the hours to a proper close. Originally, Compline wasn't even prayed in the oratory, but in the cloister where the monks live, just before they went to bed. It makes the ancient tradition of night prayers before bed a communal experience.

Compline is often listed among the Little Hours, but it is something quite by itself. It has more or less the structure of the Little Hours, but it is actually the conclusion of the whole monastic day. It starts with the prayer, "A peaceful night and a perfect end grant us." Compline connects the end of the day with the end of life itself. It reinforces the theme that the rhythm of our days parallels the rhythm of our life, and the way we live each hour, each day, determines the character of our life. The paced hours teach us how to pace our life.

Then comes the exhortation, "Be vigilant." We are warned that we are entering the night watch, when all that threatens us lurks like a prowling lion. Compline squarely faces the fearful aspect of night. It's difficult for us to imagine the fear of night that people had in earlier centuries. We just flick on the light and darkness is gone. But we know how children instinctively fear the dark, and occasionally we experience the terror of being engulfed in blackness, when the power goes out or on a hike, when we're caught after dark in the wilderness. Darkness is essentially our fear of the unknown. Just as we fear the darkness outside us, we also fear the darkness in the hidden recesses of our soul.

We confront this inner darkness at Compline by examining our conscience, asking ourselves, "What went wrong today? Where did I fail to meet the challenge?" We usually find that things go wrong because we get caught up in some response or activity without having first stopped, looked, and proceeded with deliberate clarity. Sometimes—in my experience, the rarest case—we did stop and did look, but we didn't go. What should have happened never did, because we were too sluggish to act. So we examine our conscience as we look back on the day, and ask God, the saints, and one another for forgiveness as we resolve to do better tomorrow. With that, the day is over, and we are to step deliberately into the night.

The Compline hymn with its lilting lines expresses well both the fear that grows as the light fades and the faith that grows, too, and overcomes fear.

> *Now in the fading light of day, Maker of All, to you we pray*
> *that in your ever watchful love you guard and guide us from*
> *above.*

> *Help and defend us through the night. Danger and terror put to*
> *flight.*
> *Never let evil have its way. Preserve us for another day.*

Fear is the measure of faith. There is nothing wrong with fear, as long as faith stays just a nose's length ahead of it. The greater the fear, the more glorious the courage of faith that overcomes it. In the words of the Psalmist we remind ourselves every night at Compline of the firm foundation on which our faith rests: the intimate nearness of God who says, "I rescue all who cling to me; I am with them, when they are in trouble." This intimacy is stressed by the three times repeated "my" at the beginning of the same psalm: "I can say to the Lord, 'My refuge, my fortress, my God in whom I trust!'"

THE CHARACTERISTIC PSALM for Compline is the one in which we put ourselves into the shelter of God's protecting love. As wayfarers surprised by the night might look for shelter in trees somewhere or in caves, so we go under the "wings of the Most High." Jesus speaks of God as a mother hen who gathers her chicks under her wings.

When the hymns and prayers speak of being protected from the devil who seems to have free reign in the night, we can understand the Evil One as a personification of all the negative messages we may get when we are alone in the dark. Just as angels are messengers of light, devils are those messengers of darkness who fill our imaginations with fears, frightening images, negative thoughts. We tell ourselves, "People don't really care about me" or "I'll never accomplish anything." These dark thoughts rise up out of the silence, and at Compline we seek the strength to ward them off. We chant the psalm that says "He has commanded the angels to guard you in all your ways so that you would not even dash your foot against a stone."

The night itself is, in a sense, an angel and a messenger of God's protection. Sleep is such a great gift; we know this fully only when we are sleepless or have to stay up all night. Night is at once threat and grace: threat, because when night falls, we stand at the edge of chaos—the neat little world that we have created for ourselves throughout the day now threatens to fall back into chaos; but grace also, because the protection, the divine nearness to which we have become accustomed through the chants and prayers throughout the day, will not abandon us.

In *The Book of Hours,* Rilke has a mysteriously beautiful poem in which he says, "I am returning home out of my wings, in which I lost myself." I have been consumed by activity, obsessed by movement, action, and now I am stepping out of my wings to be still. He goes on, "I was song, and God the rhyme still echoes in my ear. But now I am again growing quiet and simple, and my voice is still. I am bowing my face to a better prayer." He calls this prayer of silence "a better prayer," better at least for this hour. Compline is the hour in which we celebrate that return of song into silence, of words into silence, from which they come.

At the very end of Compline, it has become a common custom for the Abbot to bless the whole community by sprinkling them with holy water, a sort of evening dew. Then the monks file into the Lady Chapel for a final hymn to Mary. This hymn changes with the seasons. For most of the year it is *Salve Regina;* at other times, there are beautiful Marian antiphons like the *Regina Coeli* or the *Alma Redemptoris Mater,* jewels of chant.

This custom has always reminded me of children being tucked into bed at the end of the day by their mother. It brings a smile to my face to think of all these monks sweetly singing at day's end to their Mother, opening themselves to the *anima* realm of their psyche, and entrusting themselves to the infinite darkness as maternal. Thus the part of the monastery indelibly linked for me with Compline is the Lady Chapel, where we return to our spiritual womb to be reborn again next morning.

THE ANGEL OF COMPLINE has a darkish robe, with eyes closed, eyelids heavy, face bent down, hands lightly playing a small organ. Or is the angel's hand making a gesture of gentle refusal to play? This is the angel, the hour of peaceful transition into the dark silence of sleep.

FAITH IS THE VIRTUE of Compline; it is the basic trust by which we give ourselves to God's protection during the night. Just as children, frightened to face the phantasms of the night, seek their parents' assurances, at Compline we invoke our faith to give us courage amidst our terrors—real and imagined.

Compline encourages us to see with the eyes of trust that the cosmos is in fact prepared for us, like a nurturing home. We have a right to feel at home here in the universe. It has been marvelously created so as to be hospitable to human life. The central biblical theme of the Kingdom of God is an archetype of the world as God meant it to be—a place in which human beings are at home and thrive as co-creators. If we entrust ourselves to that fundamental sense of belonging to the universe, things go well, and we can make some sense even out of the worst that happens to us.

If we don't have that trust, if we give in to our fearful-ness, the worst has already happened. Then we make our-selves existential orphans in an alien world. The option to live in basic trust, to see the universe as the home that God has made for us, or to live in fear and distrust, is ultimately ours. We must choose. And this is the most important choice we make, as we live day by day. If we trust, we will be at peace; if not, we will never be.

All of our hearts ask the night this question: Am I safe and am I loved? We can mediate safety and love to one an-other. We *need* to mediate it to everyone, especially to chil-dren. If we grow up without anybody mediating this safety to us, it is hard to ever be at home in this world. We've all known unfortunate people who were never given the expe-rience of knowing safety and love. If no one helps us to ex-perience the universe as our divine home, we are all, in Robert Heinlein's arresting phrase, "strangers in a strange land."

Implicitly Compline calls us to trust in the uniqueness of each person. Personal uniqueness thrives in an atmos-phere of feeling at home and safe in the world. Most of us fear that we won't be accepted as who we are. One of

Thomas Merton's continuous and stunning admonitions to monastic communities was, "Make room for idiosyncrasies." We shouldn't accept people on condition that they conform. That's not a creative way to build community; not one that promises success. Merton knew that there could be no creativity in any community if one made conformity the criterion for belonging. The criterion for belonging must be commitment to a shared ideal, a common goal. In order to achieve that goal, we need to help one another be our best selves.

If we are to rise to the height of faith to which Compline challenges us, we must squarely face our fears by reducing them to the simple but direct question, "What is actually frightening me?" By asking this question, you give your fears some shape and definition, and this deflates their power. Nightmares have power over us only as long as they remain undefined.

Preparing for the night, for going to sleep, and for going into the realm of dreams, we pray for good dreams: nourishing dreams, teaching dreams. Sleep is a storehouse of treasures. We should enter it properly prepared. It makes all the difference in the world *how* we fall asleep.

Prepared by Compline we approach our sleeping hours with deep trust and joyful anticipation. We entrust ourselves to the night as if it were a deep ocean from which we can fish up all sorts of wonderful things. We strive to open our hearts to the blessing of rest and the promise of dreams, perhaps even meditating a bit on good things to dream about and keeping a notebook at hand to record the surprises our dreaming imagination has yielded when we wake up.

If you have children, you can bring the spirit of Compline into your home by spending some special time with them at the day's end. Soothe them with sweet stories, sing together, bless them, pray with them. Lead them from a fear of the night, which is so natural to small children, into a trust in the night as a time to merge with the loving mystery in which we are all immersed.

This gentle, deliberate ending of the day completes the circle of the hours.

THE GREAT SILENCE

SILENCE

—

THE MATRIX OF TIME

WE HAVE TRAVELED FULL CIRCLE ACROSS the seasons of the day, and have arrived at the Great Silence: the bridge of silence between Compline and Vigils that will inaugurate the cycle of the hours anew.

Music is not merely a rhythmic arrangement of notes, but derives its life from the matrix of silence out of which it arises and into which it inevitably flows. And it is the silence between the notes that gives them meaning and grace. The Great Silence is the silent rest before the day chants its recurrent melody of the hours.

When chant music stops, sometimes quite abruptly, an audible silence reverberates throughout the room, especially in the high arches of the oratories in which it is sung. This silence is not merely sound's absence, but a mysterious presence, the immense nothingness that is our origin and our home. If we listen carefully, we discover that when all is said and done, chant inducts us into this silence that is the ground of our being.

T. S. Eliot said, "Words after speech, reach into silence." This is also true of music.

Monasticism's central message, which is expressed through the chant, is the supreme importance of time and how we relate to it: how we caretake and *respond* to the present moment, to what is before us now.

The message of the hours is to live daily with the *real* rhythms of the day. To live responsively, consciously, and intentionally, directing our lives from within, not being swept along by the demands of the clock, by external agendas, by mere reactions to whatever happens. By living in the real rhythms, we ourselves become more real. We learn to listen to the music of this moment, to hear its sweet implorings, its sober directives. We learn to dance a little in our hearts, to open our inner gates a crack more, to hearken to the music of silence, the divine life breath of the universe.